Blue Peter Contents ★

Book **27**

Written by Lewis Bronze and John Comerford Co-ordinated by Anne Dixon

£4.50 UK only

A puppy reunion on **Honey's first birthday**. Honey's with John, and the other incredibly well-behaved doggies are Major, Teddy, Lily, Biddy and Margot.

John with **Liz McColgan**, world champion 10,000-metre runner, who helped launch the 1992 National Children's Fun Run.

Spot the ball! John finds that **Gary Lineker** is unbeatable even at table football – and he let in all Gary's penalties!

Hello

Welcome to the best and brightest of a wonderful Blue Peter year!

It's a year that flew by and one in which we seem to have covered every corner of the British Isles making films for Blue Peter. One of the great things about travelling so much is meeting so many people who love the programme, and finding out what they like best, or least, about it. Maybe we'll be visiting your town or school during the next year!

In our twenty-seventh Blue Peter book, you'll find the inside stories of our adventures at Jodrell Bank and cross-country skiing, meet the tallest Thunderbird puppets you're ever likely to see, and catch up on our unforgettable Summer Expedition to Japan. Then read John's reports from the Falkland Islands in the South Atlantic.

Five hundred **Girl Guides**, **Brownies** and **Rangers** from Hampshire West turned Studio One into a massive dance floor with "Tomorrow's News".

Spot the real Yvette! **Anna Peacock** won a national fashion competition by designing two outfits for her favourite personality!

*Yvette going up in the world! She was "levitated" by magician **Chris Dugdale**, but soon came down to earth.*

*Fire at Television Centre! Call for the **Old Rectory School Fire Brigade**! With too few pupils for sports teams, they have a fire brigade instead and train by putting out real fires.*

there!

Coming home again, you won't want to miss news about our two star kittens, Kari and Oke. And if you have not yet won a Blue Peter badge, turn to page 60 – we hope to hear from you soon! We've also got a Blue Peter Trivia Challenge that should settle – or start – a few arguments!

It has been a remarkable year for Blue Peter competitions – the Green stamps, the Garden Festival of Wales and Expo '92! Next year there'll be more great events and projects for you to share in.

One of the highlights of our year was being voted Best Factual Children's Programme by the British Academy of Film and Television Arts. We aim to make Blue Peter even better in 1993 – and with your help, we'll do it! So keep writing and keep watching!

*This visiting alien mudman is in fact John after finishing the practice for the **Royal Marines' Endurance Course**.*

*Well done us! The team with editor Lewis Bronze after winning the **British Academy Award** for Best Factual Children's Programme.*

*Yvette visited a **seal hospital** in Hunstanton where injured or sick seals are nursed. Yvette helped release this one back into the sea.*

A Slippin' and a

The shoot-out at the OK Corral had nothing on this! With our three presenters out to prove they're the best in the driving stakes, this race made the RAC Rally look like a fairground ride – go-karting, but on ICE!

A lot to prove for Big John, starting by showing he could actually get in the kart. Slow to get going, and lots of "accidental" bumping during the race. Took advantage of Yvette's slip to claim first place.

The race leader for nineteen of the twenty laps. Perfect control on the corners, despite excessive amounts of laughter. Terrible bad luck on the last bend led to a spin that let the others through. Final comment: "I'm gutted."

A sly one here. Lots of giggling and pretending she couldn't control the kart. Trailed behind in third place most of the time – at the last minute, overtook Yvette to come a creditable second.

Slidin'

It all happened at the John Nike Sports Centre in Bracknell. They let go-karters on their ice rink from time to time, and Blue Peter were invited along to try it out. Talk about a fight to the death! All the presenters love driving and they were all keen to prove themselves fastest.

The karts were quite nippy – capable of up to thirty miles an hour. To begin with, speed was the last thing on anyone's mind. Cornering was the tricky part, and at first they spun off at every corner, sending cones flying.

You master cornering by not trying to accelerate or brake – just give it a lot of welly on the straight bits. Yvette was the definite star, despite repeatedly being bumped from behind by a certain Scotsman.

It was terrific fun, despite Yvette's disappointment at coming third. She's suggesting hot-air balloons for our next challenge – John and Diane are reaching for their parachutes!

Plunderful

Adventures on the Spanish Main, buried treasure, pieces of eight... pirates led a romantic life.

Don't believe a word of it! They were brutes, even if they were fascinating ones. The lives of Long John Silver, Henry Morgan and Blackbeard may seem glamorous in books and films but truth has been blended with fiction.

We had terrific fun dressing up as pirates for a day and turning the studio into a pirate ship. It was to mark a special exhibition at the National Maritime Museum (always worth a visit, by the way, if you've never been).

The exhibition was called *Pirates: Fact and Fiction*. In the sections on these pages, we've played a dastardly pirate trick. In each box, there's one statement out of place. Can you spot them? *Answers are on page 61.*

FACT (probably!)

1 Port Royal, the pirate capital in Jamaica, was named the "wickedest city in the world".

2 Annie Bonny was a woman pirate, as fearsome and brave as any. Her husband, Jack Rackham, died on the gallows. Annie escaped the hangman.

3 There are pirates today. Instead of the Jolly Roger and cutlasses, they're equipped with radar and machine guns. They attack oil tankers, refugees and fishing boats.

Pirates!

4 In Queen Elizabeth I's time, English captains like Sir Francis Drake were given permission to attack Spanish ships and steal their cargoes of gold. Really they were little better than pirates.

5 One of the most famous mutinies ever was when the pirate crew of the Hispaniola took over its ship.

FICTION (definitely!)

1 The most famous fictional pirate must be Long John Silver in Treasure Island by Robert Louis Stevenson.

2 The pirate Blackbeard used to terrify his enemies by going into battle with smoking fuses in his hair.

3 Another famous pirate, Captain Hook from Peter Pan, helps Britain's most famous children's hospital, Great Ormond Street. The author, J M Barrie, gave his earnings from the story to the hospital.

4 In Hook, Dustin Hoffman wears his hook on the wrong arm!

5 Swallows and Amazons by Arthur Ransome is all about pirates in the Lake District.

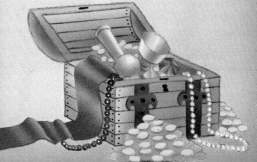

How's this for a rags-to-riches story? One two-day-old kitten, left to die in a hedge, was rescued by an animal sanctuary and six weeks later appeared before millions of viewers on Blue Peter!

That is the story of Oke, the male half of our new pair of kittens. Kari, the female, also came from the Wood Green Animal Shelter. Her mother had been abandoned with her litter of three newborn kittens, and the motherless Oke was given to her to nurse.

When John and vet Bradley Viner went to the shelter to look for new kittens for the programme, they found the pair very appealing. We'd decided to have non-pedigree animals on Blue Peter for a change, hoping they might be less highly strung and happier in a television studio – Willow sometimes lost her temper and we felt it was unfair to make her appear on television any longer.

Bradley also thought two kittens would be good because they could keep each other company. Once we'd seen those adorable kittens, nobody disagreed!

Their unusual names take some explaining. At the time, John and Diane's films from Japan were being shown, and about half a dozen viewers made an inspired choice: Kari (for the female) and Oke (for the male) after Karaoke, the singalong Japanese music machine so memorably tried out by John and Diane.

Kari and Oke love to wander around the studio. They are inquisitive but *very* well behaved. We hope they'll be starring on Blue Peter for many years!

Oke loves making friends and playing with toys, especially his fish-on-a-line. He'll happily sit on your lap for ages – as long as he's getting a good stroking!

CARING FOR YOUR KITTENS

*Besides making sure kittens have a few toys to enjoy, and perhaps a **scratching post**, there's a lot you can do to make sure that your kitten is happy and healthy. Far too many unwanted cats end up as strays. Many have to be put to sleep. Unless you want to breed from your pet, you should ask your vet about **neutering**. This minor operation means that your cat will not be able to become a father or a mother to kittens.*

WOOD GREEN SHELTER

If you want a kitten or a puppy, and you are sure you can do all the hard work needed to look after it, then an **animal shelter** like Wood Green's three branches may be able to help you. They'll ask lots of questions to find out if you can offer a pet a good home, and they'll make sure the animal is neutered, hoping to cut down on the number of abandoned cats and dogs that they and other animal charities have to care for.

Kari, the female, is the more mischievous of the two. Just getting her to sit still long enough for a photo is quite an achievement!

LEUCOGEN

Kari and Oke were among the first kittens in the country to receive doses of a new vaccine that will eliminate one of the deadliest and commonest of all cat diseases – **feline leukaemia**. The vaccine's been in use for some time in France and the United States but has only recently been brought to Britain.

11

To boldly go...

Captain's log: Stardate 29 46.3

We have reached the twenty-fifth year of our five-year mission. We have encountered all manner of fearsome aliens. But no mission, no aliens, can match our awful experience in the sector of the universe known as BBC Television Centre, when our physical beings and our brain patterns were temporarily possessed by that strange lifeform known as "Blue Peter presenters".

What weird universe can these beings inhabit? Even Spock, never one to reveal emotion, was quaking in the transporter room when Scottie finally managed to beam us back aboard the *Enterprise*.

None of this would have happened if Uhura had not broadcast on all hailing frequencies that the *Enterprise* and her crew were celebrating that fateful twenty-fifth anniversary. Those alien presenters consume anniversaries as other species eat food. Their S.M.A.C. (super-magnetic anniversary collector) just sucked us in from six galaxies away.

Thankfully, it's over. We can continue to boldly go. And next time we have an anniversary, I'm going to make sure Bones gives Uhura a sedative!

What has been your biggest mistake?
Almost killing myself falling asleep while driving my car when I was eighteen.

Who is your favourite musician?
Les Dawson playing the piano! Only kidding – Jean-Michel Jarre.

What are the main advantages and disadvantages of being so tall?
Advantages: Playing sport and seeing the action at concerts or football grounds.
Disadvantages: Can't find clothes or shoes that will fit.

What is your best sporting memory?
1990: Scotland beating England at Murrayfield to win the Five-Nations Championship.

Since you joined Blue Peter, which personal achievement has given you most pleasure?
Completing the London Marathon.

What don't you eat?
Indian food, shellfish and liver.

When you were younger, which comics did you read?
"The Victor" and "Hotspur".

John Leslie

Who, besides your parents, has been the most influential figure in your life so far?
I learn from watching very good television presenters. And Sean Connery is the epitome of a true Scots gent!

Which foreign country would you like to live in? (England does not count here!)
USA.

Please highlight the words that describe you:
Creative Musical Artistic Loving Stern Forgiving Intolerant Solitary **Determined** Undecided **Enthusiastic** Charming

Birthday: **February 22nd**
Star sign: **Pisces**
Height: **6' 5"**
Colour of eyes: **Blue**
Colour of hair: **Brown**
Joined Blue Peter: **April 1989**
Job before starting: **Television presenter for a satellite station.**

JAPAN

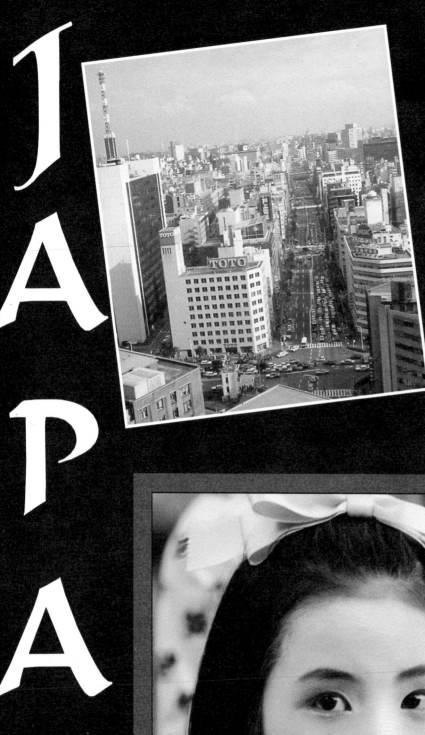

Sushi and small beds – if it weren't for those, Japan would be John's kind of place!

Speeding into Tokyo from Narita Airport on board the luxurious airport express, you catch your first glimpse of the ultra-modern Japanese way of life. The computerised route map pinpoints your position as the densely populated suburbs of the *vast* capital race past, and the day's news stories are flashed up on a carriage screen. Hi-tech touches like this are the norm in Japan – the nation that's living out the world's vision of the future today.

Nearly twelve million people live in the Tokyo metropolis – enough to make you feel completely peopled out – but somehow it isn't quite like that. Sure it's crowded, but the city works like clockwork. It has one of the best city transport systems in the world, which makes life easy for the millions of commuters.

Sushi · Bonsai · Hi-tech

People are polite – no one pushes, they just go about their business with a quiet determination. With so many people and so little space, Tokyo has made use of some clever ideas to fit it all in – such as capsule hotels with rooms or slots just big enough to fit a body (but not quite so good if you're Leslie sized!), golf driving ranges on roof tops, and sky-parks – automatic car parking in narrow towers.

You don't find as many old buildings in Tokyo as in most European capitals. People and nature have heaped disasters on it. With earthquakes, fires and bombings, it's been destroyed twice this century alone. But in each case it has rebuilt itself with typical Japanese efficiency. Tokyo today is a vibrant, buzzing place – not the most beautiful city, but one you never forget.

Behind the Japan of electronic gadgets, bullet trains and futuristic cars, there is a country that's steeped in ancient tradition.

The Japanese are proud of their history and try to keep their culture alive.

In the ancient city of Kyoto, with shrines and temples on every corner, you come face to face with old Japan. Step off the street into one of the beautiful Buddhist temple gardens and you are a million miles from the bustle of modern Japan. The garden is more than somewhere to sit – it's a place to think and meditate. ▶

Children take part in the traditional life of the country with enthusiasm. In Kyoto we came across a group celebrating the festival of Gion Matsuri. Children as young as five were dressed in fabulously colourful costumes, with faces painted white with bright red lips. They danced with slow, serious and dignified movements and went on to process through the streets of the city to traditional, haunting Japanese music played on the drum and flute.

This is Blue Peter in Japanese!

JAPAN

◀ Putting on the kimono is an art in itself. It is supposed to represent harmony with nature.

▼ Meet an unusual Samurai warrior! John appeared in a Japanese answer to Neighbours.

It was here that Diane stepped into the past and put on traditional Japanese dress. The kimono is an artform. The beauty is in the design and texture of the fabric, a reflection of nature, rather than the cut; there are no zips or buttons and it's held together by a sash called an "obi". These days the graceful kimono is worn only on formal occasions.

School children work hard in Japan. There is tremendous pressure in the classroom and at home to do well. In the southern island of Kyushu, we visited a school where the pupils have another difficulty to cope with. The school lives in the shadow of a volcano.

In Japan earthquakes and volcanic eruptions are a part of everyday life. Sakurajima, one of 160 volcanoes (most of which lie dormant), is home to several thousand people living on its slopes. Their security is in the hands of scientists, who constantly monitor the volcano. There's also the daily problem of how to live

The monument to Sadako, a victim of radiation sickness, who died ten years after the atomic bomb destroyed her home, Hiroshima. Our visit here was the most moving of our expedition. Sadako thought that if she folded a thousand paper cranes, she would be cured, but she did not finish. Today children from all over the world send cranes in the name of peace.

with the massive quantity of ash that the volcano belches out.

The local children have learned to live with the ash and the fear of the next blast. Evacuation drills are as regular a feature of the school timetable as Maths. There's also a vital school uniform accessory – a crash helmet! Japan is a country of contrasts: remote mountain ranges and teeming neon-lit cities, Samurai warriors and grey-suited businessmen, ancient and new, traditional and modern. The Land of the Rising Sun fascinates and confuses – just when you think you're getting to know it, it throws up something completely unexpected.

ラルーピーター

Viva
ESPAÑA!

Viva Seifert, the girl with the grace of a ballerina, the skill of a juggler and the strength of a gymnast, has the world at her feet. The day she visited Blue Peter, she took time off from her punishing training schedule for the Barcelona Olympic Games.

Nineteen-year-old Viva was the 1991 British Rhythmic Gymnastics Champion. It's a sport that combines ballet, gymnastics and juggling skills and has five different disciplines involving either rope, hoop, ball, clubs or ribbon. Viva's favourite is the clubs. To give herself the best chance of a gold medal at the Olympics, she travelled to Moscow to be trained by a Russian coach. "The Russians have the best team in the world and the best coaches," Viva explained. It's an extremely demanding sport, and Viva practises for up to ten hours each day before major competitions.

The long hours would seem to have paid off. The performance she gave on the

programme was breathtaking. Working to a Spanish-style flamenco piece of music, she moved about the studio floor, twirling and swirling the clubs with natural rhythm and poise. Her lean physique made magnificent shapes and graceful sweeps. Breathlessness at the end of her display was the only sign of how difficult the sport is. She made it look so easy!

John asked her how much of the display she made up herself. "Quite a lot, but the choreography and choice of music is a team effort from my coach and club-mates. The original throws and catches you dream up yourself because they give you extra points."

After the Barcelona Olympics, Britain's young hopeful intends to retire to concentrate on more academic interests – a university degree course. Rhythmic Gymnastics' loss is Edinburgh University's gain!

I'm dreaming of a

Clare holds a licence for using a chainsaw. Nice to know you're in an expert's hands when the chips are flying!

Diane laid into that tree trunk with the help of well-known green person Bill Oddie. The trunk never stood a chance!

Chopped up and stripped of branches, the mighty tree looked somehow even bigger. Two lorries were needed to transport it.

In the Blue Peter garden, the trunk was sawn into logs, which in turn were thwacked into smaller pieces with a splitter.

Green Christmas

Is there a Christmas tree in your home right now? Since lots of people first read their Blue Peter annual around Christmas, it's a fair bet the answer is yes. And if it's a real tree, what are you planning to do with it once Twelfth Night arrives? Put it out for the dustmen?

You could do something that will help the environment instead. Copy what we did with Britain's most famous Christmas tree – recycle it!

The Trafalgar Square tree is an annual gift to the people of Britain from the people of Norway. Each year, a magnificent Norwegian spruce is sent to Britain to stand proudly in the heart of the capital. And each year, on January 6th, the tree is thrown away.

Until 1992, that is. For the first time, Westminster City Council decided to do something more useful with their unwanted tree, and they asked Blue Peter to help them.

Clare and Diane helped chop up the tree and bring it to Television Centre. You couldn't move that day in the Blue Peter garden for hi-tech tree-choppers. In no time, one forty-metre-high spruce was reduced to one very large pile of chippings.

And that's the recycling part. Chippings make mulch, once they've been allowed to rot down for a year or so. Then the mulch gets spread on the garden, putting all its nutrients back into the soil.

You could do the same with your tree. Find out if your local council or garden centre is running a Christmas tree recycling scheme, so that your tree will be doing some good long after the fairy has been packed away for another year.

The end result! Masses of fresh tree chips, ready to make lovely organic compost.

21

This button *(left)* can be a lifeline, allowing an elderly person to call for emergency help. Specially adapted minibuses *(below)* can be better than public transport if you can't manage big steps. And a home laundry service, like this one in Belfast *(bottom)*, is a real help for incontinent people.

"It's like a palace compared to the place we used to be in."

"I used to live alone – I don't any more. It's as if I've someone with me twenty-four hours a day."

Just two comments from elderly people who have benefited from the 1991 Blue Peter Golden Age Appeal. The second was made by Isla Douglas of Durham about her Lifeline Alarm telephone. Eighty-one years old and blind, she's still able to live in confidence in her own home because she wears a special necklace that has a red button on it. This can put her in touch with a control centre. They know where she is and who to contact in an emergency.

The first comment was made by John Black in Belfast, about the larger house his day centre is able to move into thanks to a grant from Help the Aged, provided by Blue Peter viewers through the Appeal.

We chose the elderly to benefit from the 1991 Blue Peter Appeal because it was nineteen years since we had last held an appeal to help old people. That's too long to ignore a growing number of people who can so easily be forgotten by the young and healthy.

A real problem for many elderly people is incontinence. That means not being able to control when you go to the lavatory. Most elderly people suffer alone, because they are embarrassed to tell anyone about it.

It's strange to compare a baby with an elderly person. Everyone knows a baby isn't able to use a lavatory, and there are hundreds of kinds of nappies, baby wipes and so on. When did you last see an advert for an elderly person's incontinence pad? We thought our viewers, many of whom have baby brothers and sisters, would understand the problem.

We were right. The aluminium cans poured in, each one worth over a penny to the Appeal. With the money raised from nineteen million cans, Help the Aged will be helping to set up the country's first combined home laundry and incontinence advice service. They are also providing two minibuses in Manchester and Rochester, a hundred Lifeline Alarm telephones and a control centre, improved day centres in Belfast and Abroath, and a Care and Repair advice service in South Wales.

Blue Peter viewers proved once again that they care and can work hard to reach an Appeal target. We were delighted to show that there's a special link between the young and the old. With a bit of love and care, old age *can* be a Golden Age.

Everyone at Macduff Primary School *(above)* in Banff collected cans – so did their chip shop! They were taken to a Wm Low supermarket. All your Golden Age cans went to Warrington to be recycled *(below)*.

CHIN-wagging

Yuck! Remember the day those ugly old crones took over Blue Peter? With their bald heads and yack-yacking mouths, we thought they would never leave!

And their friends! There was Ginnochio, the old man with the red nose, and that funny foot guy. Simply the weirdest people you *ever* met.

Actually, you could meet them too – in your very own bedroom. All you need are some simple make-up bits and pieces, and a couple of scraps of material. Then you can create your own madcap family of characters.

The faces are painted upside-down chins. It's amazing how your chin can turn into a little person with a mind of its own when it's upside-down. Just dab on the eyes and a nose and let your mouth do the talking. It's weird!

And with a bit more imagination, you can copy the tremendously original skills of the mime artists we met, Ines and Hugo. Ines is the foot person and Hugo is Ginnochio, the knee. Don't get fooled into thinking all you have to do is dress up as they do – that's only the start. The real genius of their art is in the movements they give their characters, which are so clever that when you're watching, you forget it's a knee or a foot and really believe you are looking at a person.

Maybe you can do even better!

"Diane-Louise, she's such a show-off, I mean what kind of name is Diane-Louise, what's wrong with Ethel, it was good enough for my auntie and she lived to be one hundred and two? Kept playing MC Hammer on her kazoo, mind you, but there was nothing wrong with our Ethel that a complete oil change wouldn't have put right..."

See how Ines twisted and bent her foot to give her little man a mind of his own. A black cloth for a background will help the effect!

"Ooohh, and that Yvette, she's no better, always dressing up and putting on funny voices. What's she got to be so proud about, that's what I'd like to know ... what do they mean by keeping us hanging about like this? Isn't it time for Blue Peter yet?"

Who looks rather wooden, is held up by strings and sometimes has trouble matching his lips with the words? John Leslie?

Wrong! That's a rude way of describing the most unlikely new stars on television this year – the crew of International Rescue, who roam the world getting people out of tight spots and keeping the evil Hood at bay.

Of course, they're not "new" at all. In fact, they're a lot older than most Blue Peter viewers.

Thunderbirds' creator, Gerry Anderson (left), is delighted that his characters are still going strong. Thanks to the skill of the original puppeteers (below), the characters' limbs, heads, eyes and even lips can move.

International Rescue first appeared on British television in the late 1960s. Their space-age vehicles (long before the Shuttle was off the drawing board) were a big hit with viewers.

But even Gerry Anderson, creator of Thunderbirds, must have thought the series' glory days were over once the special effects of *Star Wars* and computer-driven entertainment replaced puppets on strings.

When he came to the programme, he said he was amazed but delighted by Thunderbirds' success among a new generation of viewers. Over five million people are making a date with Scott, Virgil, Gordon, Alan, Brains, Lady Penelope and Parker.

BIRDS ARE GO!

Everyone has their favourite Thunderbird character. Many of us on Blue Peter are fans of Lady P – secretly we'd all like to be invited to take tea with her, served, of course, by the finest of butlers, Parker.

The renewed success of the programme led to a search for one of its stars. Virgil Tracey was missing – unlike the other puppets, he had not been saved when the series ended. He turned up in a loft of all places. A quick-witted fan had rescued Virgil from a skip – a case of the rescuer rescued. After repairs, he's now fine again.

The only pity is, they don't plan to make any new episodes. Perhaps they should send for International Rescue!

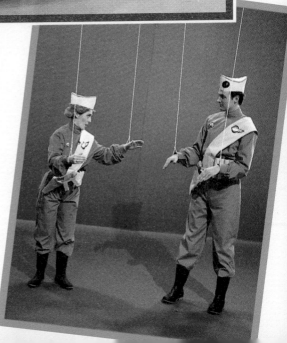

The real FAB 1 (above), Lady Penelope's pink Rolls, was authentic Thunderbirds, but was this character (left) one of the Tracey brothers? John and Yvette (right) got all tied up getting into the role of Scott and Alan, but found there were strings attached!

Penguin Paradise

◄ Stanley is the Islands' capital. No larger than a British village, it is home to about a thousand people.

▼ Guess who was interviewed by local children for their very own radio programme, *Out and About*?

Did you ever visit somewhere and have the feeling that you had been there before?

That was how I felt in the Falkland Islands. I had travelled eight thousand miles to the South Atlantic, but once there, I felt as if I was off the coast of Scotland.

Except, that is, for the penguins. Rockhoppers, jackasses, king – they love the Falklands. They let you walk right up to them and scarcely bat a tailfeather. They all thrive on the rocky shores and marshland of the two hundred or more islands that make up the Falklands.

Wildlife could be a key to the future of the Islands, because tourists will pay to see this unspoiled paradise. Traditional sheep farming is in decline and Falkland Islands wool does not fetch the high price it once did.

There are only about 1,900 people living on the Falklands. Some live in isolated settlements, like Sammy Lee, who lives on a sheep farm on Pebble Island. Sammy has most of her lessons over the two-way radio, with a teacher fifty miles away. Sammy loves the life. She looks after ducks, sheep and ponies and, if she fancies a swim, she can dive into one of the crystal-clear pools nearby.

For Islanders older than thirteen, the main event of their lives has been the invasion by Argentina in

Watching Blue Peter in the town hall. Children on the Falklands see Blue Peter a week later than in Britain. Seems to be quite popular!

anyone could fight in such a remote and beautiful land. There are still no links between the Islands and Argentina, their nearest neighbour.

One reminder of the war still poses a threat – the unexploded mines left on many beaches. The areas are fenced off but the penguins don't seem to mind. They're too small to set the bombs off, so they wander freely through the safest bird reserves in the world!

▲ Memories of the war of 1982 are very fresh for Anna Robson. She was one of 114 Islanders held while the battle of Goose Green raged around them.

1982. At the tenth anniversary of the British victory and the Islands' liberation, memories were still very fresh.

I followed the course of the war, visiting "Bomb Alley" at San Carlos Water, where the Royal Navy fought off air attacks; Goose Green, where the 2nd Battalion of the Parachute Regiment defeated a force three times their size; and the mountains that hold the approach to Stanley – all scenes of desperate and bloody fighting.

It was strange to think that

▲ Sammy Lee in her very own classroom. Usually she talks to her teacher over the radio.

◄ There are many more sheep than people on the Falklands. This poor sheep won't forget John's visit! Thankfully, it lived to tell the tale.

The thing that's odd about pancakes is this – why only once a year? They are so yummy, you could have them every week and not be bored. Never mind if it's months till Shrove Tuesday – have a go at the recipes here. They're dead easy.

To start, you need your **basic pancake mixture:**

125g plain flour
2 eggs lightly beaten
pinch of salt
1 tablespoon vegetable oil or melted butter
125 ml (half a pint) of milk
This should make about ten pancakes – eight if you're greedy!

Sieve the flour and salt into a bowl. Make a little dip in the middle and pour the beaten egg and the oil into it. Gradually beat in the milk a little at a time until the batter is smooth and creamy. Leave the mixture alone for about 30 minutes.

That's the way to do it! John is most impressed by Stephen Yates' stylish toss.

To cook the pancakes, heat a little butter or oil in a frying pan. When it's so hot it's steaming, carefully pour in a little batter. Swirl it around and cook it until the pancake's brown. Be brave – have a good toss! Cook the other side. You've just become a pancake maker – well done!

Savoury filling:
Cut two or three bacon rashers into small pieces and fry with some chopped onion until crisp. Put some filling in a cooked pancake, roll it up, and then grate some cheese on top. Bake in the oven or put under the grill until the cheese melts.

Suggested by Stephen Yates.

Re-decorate your ceiling

...hose girls. Ask them to toss a pancake
...stepladder trying to scrape an ugly looking mess
...don't know their own strengths!

Sweet fillings:
Here are two suggested by viewers.

Banana and butterscotch sauce
1½ tablespoons golden syrup
2 tablespoons brown sugar
2 tablespoons single cream
lump of butter
2 drops vanilla essence
banana slices

Mix the syrup, sugar and butter together in a saucepan on a low heat until the sugar melts. Carefully bring to the boil for two minutes. Take off the heat, add cream and vanilla essence, then serve inside the pancake, with the banana slices.

Recipe from Julia Barnett.

Orange pancakes
Instead of using milk in the batter, use orange juice and stir in the finely grated rind of half an orange.
Serve your pancakes with some orange segments inside and some natural yoghurt or ice cream on top. Megayumdrops!

Recipe from David Lees.

Take extra care with hot fat. Ask an adult to help.

Chef Leslie picks up some juicy tips from pancake maker Julia Barnett.

with Diane and Yvette...

When I was a little girl, I remember my Dad pointing out the giant metal dish we used to pass by. "I helped build that," he used to say, with more than a hint of pride.

The dish is the Jodrell Bank Radio Telescope used by astronomers to probe deep space. For the last twenty-eight years, it has dominated the Cheshire countryside near Macclesfield, a single massive ear listening to the emptiness of space.

So I was looking forward to my assignment to help repaint it. It wasn't too bad standing inside the dish. It's tilted so it points straight up. Walking in it is a bit like being a pea rolling around a gigantic bowl.

The fun started when I had to pop out of a window and dangle from the end of a rope to paint the supports. Safety harness securely on, I felt myself being lowered into nothingness. "Courage," thought I, "remember the family tradition." And with my paintbrush at arm's length, I began to daub the metal legs with their fresh coat of white paint. And that's how I became the second member of the Fielding family to work on the Jodrell Bank Radio Telescope!

The main radio telescope at Jodrell Bank stands thirty metres high, and it's got to be kept gleaming white. Don't ask me why. Guess who got the job!

Don't look down!

If you keep smiling, nobody can see what's happening inside your tummy! Judging from this picture, I'd done the difficult bit of clambering out of the window, but I can't see how I managed to paint with my hands gripping that girder!

What makes you happy?
Going into the the countryside with the family, working in the garden, and being with my husband, Barry.

What do you like to do on a day off?
Sometimes I like to do nothing. Other days, I shop, go for walks or see friends.

Would you like to have children, and how many do you think would suit you?
Yes, I think two would do just fine.

If you had not joined Blue Peter, what do you think you would be doing now?
Something on stage.

If you could live anywhere in the world, where would you choose?
On a farm in the middle of nowhere in Wales.

Which items are you never without?
My diary, purse, door keys, tissues, lots of make-up.

What is your professional ambition?
To be successful singing and dancing on the stage.

Yvette Fielding

Please highlight the words that describe you:
Thoughtful Shy **Impulsive** Brave **Funny** Beautiful **Warm** Ambitious Private **Determined Friendly** Fit

What sort of people do you most dislike?
Arrogant, selfish, unhappy people.

Who is your favourite rock star?
Madonna.

Birthday: **23rd September**
Star sign: **Libra**
Height: **5′ 4″**
Colour of eyes: **Blue/grey**
Colour of hair: **Light brown**
Joined Blue Peter: **1987**
Job before starting: **Dental nurse**

33

The FLYING SCOT
(with one foot on the ground)

Thirty tonnes of metal, with hydraulics and electronics – capable of climbing to a dizzy forty thousand feet, flying supersonic at more than two thousand miles per hour, or simply hovering three metres off the ground. For such an unaerodynamic lump, it's very agile, but what's really astonishing is that it does its stuff without ever leaving the ground.

The secret is that it gives the impression of doing all these things. Pilots have learned to fly on simulators for years now, but this piece of kit goes a step further. It is used to help scientists find better ways of laying out controls in the cockpit and to test new aircraft. The clever bit is that, with a minor adjustment, it can be anything from the latest jet fighter to a helicopter!

When the Defence Research Agency gave Blue Peter special permission to try out the new technology, John 'Biggles' Leslie didn't need to be asked twice.

"I feel like an astronaut," John exclaimed, togged up for his first appointment with a jet fighter. The control room commands came over the headset: "Push forward on the throttle half an inch – OK – 3, 2, 1 – you have control." With that the aircraft roared off into the sky. It was almost impossible to believe it was nothing but illusion.

"It's an amazing sensation, you really believe you're going to hit the hillside." Seconds later, those words were to come true! Undeterred, with a few leaves in the undercarriage, Flight Lieutenant Leslie was airborne again. A series of violent rolls, dives and climbs, and the runway was in sight. Descent and approach looked good. Touchdown! But the slippery aircraft overshot... it's not as easy as it looks!

With flights in the simulator costing thirty times less than the real thing, no environmental threat to consider and no one to complain about the noise of low flying, the machine is proving popular – not least with one Blue Peter presenter who has his sights set on Top Gun!

▼ Five, four three, two, one, full thrust... Visor down and ready to go, John's journey into the make-believe world of the simulator is just a moment away.

▲ Wearing the right kit is all part of the illusion. Helmet and tackle on, John is equipped for the flight. All that remains is to be pushed into the heart of the operation – the cockpit.

OO-ER!!

WOW!!

▲ From the outside the pumping hydraulics throw the simulator into a series of death-defying moves – climbing and diving, loop-the-looping and rolling.

▲ A righthand bank successfully completed and BP's own fighter pilot is getting to grips with the slippery Tornado. "Just a moment – I think I'm upside down!"

EXPO '92 SEVILLA

The Fiesta

For six months in 1992, Seville played host to the biggest party the world has ever seen. ¡Hola! Bienvenue! Wilkommen! Hello! Welcome to Expo!

The Spanish had been building and planning Expo for over ten years. In that time they turned a desolate, mosquito-ridden swampy island into the most amazing, massive exhibition site. They

Expo combined old and new – a beautifully restored fifteenth-century monastery and one of the stunning new bridges linking the island site with the city of Seville.

A section (left) of one of the stars of the show – the water wall on the British Pavilion. This giant perspex structure (below) towered over European Avenue and represented all the nations of the European Community.

built motorways, a new airport and a high-speed rail link from Madrid. In Seville itself, they built seven new bridges to link the island with the city.

The site, with a restored monastery that became a royal palace, featured a television screen the size of a three-storey house, a monorail, the world's first air- conditioned cable-car, and the biggest wall of water in the world (on the British Pavilion). One of the things that was most interesting was the attention paid to detail. The lamp-posts, the litter bins, even the perimeter fence had all been specially designed.

One hundred countries came to the Expo party, bringing their best and brightest to show off to the rest of the world. Visitors came in their millions from all over the world to gaze at pavilions the size of cathedrals, and to enjoy the dancing, music and spectacle of thousands of live events.

Some pavilions looked like fairy castles or eastern temples; ▶

EXPO '92 SEVILLA

Images of Expo... a trick of the eye on the Swiss Pavilion (right). The circle was actually in many different parts, painted on the backgrounds. It appeared as a circle viewed from one spot only.

some were modern glass and steel constructions.

The Spanish certainly know how to organise a party. Even the entry tickets said a lot about them – Expo was open until four in the morning!

A modern-day Sphinx? Actually, an alpine horn from Switzerland (left). The sun (below left) was part of a display in the British Pavilion. The Japanese claimed their pavilion (below) was the largest wooden structure in the world.

Blue Peter became involved nearly two years before Expo opened in April 1992. The organisers of the British Pavilion came to us because they wanted a child to design one of the displays inside.

Taking the future of the planet as a theme, they wanted ideas for a giant circular display that would be animated. That's to say, it would have moving parts. When we launched the competition in January 1992,

Yvette described it as "designing a picture on a giant mint-with-a-hole."

The overall competition winner turned out to be Sarah Hawryla, an eight-year-old from Shipley in West Yorkshire. Her design for a world in which there's enough food for all, where the scars on the environment are healed, where rusty tanks are used by birds for nests, where cars are wind-powered, gave a wonderful idea of the future, and it was funny too!

In the hands of professional model-makers Derek and Kit Freeborn, Sarah's design became a magnificent display. Sarah could hardly believe it when she visited the workshop. As promised, all the parts that could move did! The whale chased the fishermen, the chicks cheeped, the waste monster thumped himself on the head and continued to do so for the six months of Expo!

When the Blue Peter team went filming at Expo in April, we were very proud to see Sarah's display in such a prominent position inside the British Pavilion.

For those lucky enough to visit Expo, it was probably a once-in-a-lifetime experience. There certainly will not be another Expo like this until after the year 2000. It was a place where, for a few months, the world showed off all its good things – not to make money, just to make friends. War, poverty, abuse of human rights, cruelty, disease: we all know far too much of those awful things exists. They were not invited to the Expo '92 fiesta. In Seville in 1992, for a few months, they were forgotten, making way for the biggest party the world has ever seen. And we're delighted Blue Peter was there!

39

THE ★★★★★★★★★★★★★
Blue Peter TRIVIA
CHALLENGE!

EASY

1 Which city did John grow up in?

2 Which of the current presenters joined the team first?

3 Which presenters went on the Summer Expedition to Zimbabwe?

4 And which ones went to the West Coast of the USA?

5 How many aluminium cans were finally collected in the Golden Age Appeal?

HARD

6 Name at least four of Bonnie's six pups.

7 To the nearest half-million pounds, how much money did the Great Bring and Buy for Romania raise?

8 Who edited Blue Peter for twenty-seven years?

9 Which ex-Blue Peter presenter is often found on Radio Five?

10 Which ex-Blue Peter presenter is often found on Radio Four?

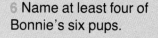

Lots of people think they know about Blue Peter. We think this trivia quiz should sort out the real experts. When we tried it, Diane was the winner with 17 marks, but Yvette thinks she cheated!

VIRTUALLY IMPOSSIBLE

16 What was the name of Percy Thrower's home?

17 What *is* the blue peter?

18 Which ex-presenter was Charlie Chaplin?

19 Which ex-presenter was Oliver Hardy?

20 Which presenter was Stan Laurel?

MEGA-HARD

11 Which ex-Blue Peter presenter is often found on Radio Bedfordshire?

12 Which drama college did Diane attend? (You'll only know if you read the last annual.)

13 What class of locomotive is the 60532 Blue Peter?

14 What car did Diane drive to Brighton?

15 Which brass band always joins us for our Christmas programme?

THIS ONE'S A LULU

21 What connection do Fairway and Fancy Free have with Blue Peter?

If you get all these right without looking at the answers on page 61, then you spend far too much time watching television!

1958

1988

great ball of GAS!

If anyone offers you a day return trip to Neptune, check that it's not April 1st! It would take you at least twelve years to get there, and the only thing to have visited it so far is the unmanned space probe, Voyager 2.

What a visit! It was almost worth waiting thousands of years and a dozen civilizations. During Voyager 2's brief fly-by, the giant planet offered up some of its secrets: many more moons than astronomers believed – eight, not two; rings, like Saturn but not as spectacular; and what winds! If you think Dartmoor or North Yorkshire are windy places, you'll need more than an anorak on Neptune. Wind speeds can be as high as 1,600 kph (1,000 mph).

Astronomer John Mason came to Blue Peter following a conference in Arizona, USA where scientists discussed and analysed the millions of facts about Neptune sent back by Voyager 2. Space items are among the most popular we do on Blue Peter, and astronomers like John, Heather Couper and Patrick Moore make regular appearances when there's something new to show or talk about.

▶ A close-up view of Neptune's mysterious Great Dark Spot, which is as large as our planet Earth. Scientists think that the Spot is a huge storm system spinning in an anticlockwise direction.

▼ The illustration below shows the comparative sizes of the sun and planets in our Solar System.

WHY IS NEPTUNE SO BLUE?
Not because it's made up of clean water. The blueness is caused by some of the giant clouds and a gas called methane.

MERCURY VENUS EARTH MARS JUPITER SATURN URANUS NEPTUNE

SUN

Triton is Neptune's largest moon and the coldest place in the entire Solar System – just minus 235°C! That's below the temperature that the gas nitrogen becomes a liquid and freezes solid. Part of Triton is covered in pink snow!

NO SURFACE TO WALK ON

Could men and women ever visit Neptune? Besides the time it would take to get there, landing would be a problem – you'd need a spacecraft carrying a Thunderbird 4-type submarine. The surface is gas or liquid, not solid. It would be incredibly difficult to find a craft that could stand up to those strong winds. There are no plans for a manned flight, but NASA hope to send another unmanned probe to Neptune as part of the Pluto Fly-by/Neptune Orbiter mission, but that will not be for at least another thirty years! Perhaps if your children watch Blue Peter in 2021, they'll tell you about it!

THE LONELY SPACECRAFT

Voyager 2 is an explorer to match Christopher Columbus or David Livingstone. Launched in August 1977, well before most Blue Peter viewers were born, it has flown past Jupiter, Saturn, Uranus and Neptune – the only spacecraft to have visited the last two so far. The instruments on board have allowed scientists on Earth to make many discoveries about our fellow planets in the Solar System. Voyager 2 continues its journey into the depths of outer space, speeding on at 14.8 kilometres each second (9.2 miles per second.) In just over forty thousand years it will pass a nearby star. Don't wait up!

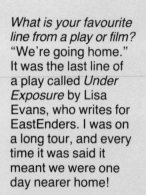

IN THE HOT SEAT

...like to present?
Woman's Hour on Radio 4.

Which part of your body gives you the most grief, and why?
My mouth – I often talk before I think!

What is your favourite line from a play or film?
"We're going home."
It was the last line of a play called *Under Exposure* by Lisa Evans, who writes for EastEnders. I was on a long tour, and every time it was said it meant we were one day nearer home!

Which is your favourite Shakespeare play?
A Midsummer Night's Dream.

What is the greatest luxury you could ever wish for?
Contentment.

What has been your proudest moment on Blue Peter?
When we raised £6,500,000 for Romania!

Which cartoon character are you most like?
Dick Dastardly – because he's sly and cunning!

Diane-Louise Jordan

Please highlight the words that describe you:
Stubborn Cheeky **Modest**
Perceptive Organised
Creative Friendly Sharp
Emotional Extravagant
Reliable Tough Sensible

If you could do any job at all for six months, what would it be and why?
I'd work in an Easter-egg factory because I love chocolate!

Who is your favourite female musician?
Caron Wheeler.

Birthday: **February 27th**
Star sign: **Pisces**
Height: **5′ 0″**
Colour of eyes: **Brown**
Colour of hair: **Black**
Joined Blue Peter: **January 1990**
Job before starting: **Presenting the television programme: Corners.**

STAMPS of SUCCESS!

Blue Peter viewers get up to all sorts of things, but even by our high standards, designing a set of Britain's stamps counts as something truly remarkable.

In 1991, the Royal Mail came to Blue Peter with their idea. They wanted to bring out their first set of "green" stamps, devoted to the environment and conservation, in 1992. And they wanted children to design them.

It's not every day you get the chance to do something that will be seen by millions of people. In fact 27,256 viewers sent designs and twelve winners were chosen. That's because the Royal Mail were not prepared to alter their strict rules. All new sets are designed by *three* artists, but only one is chosen. Our twelve winning designs were passed to three professional designers, and we were delighted when the four given to designer Lynn Trickett were selected.

Well done to Sarah Jo, Lewis, Alice and Christopher!

▼ Designer:
Christopher Hall,
aged 9
Judges' comment:
The black oil drops are a wonderful way of showing acid rain, and the flower says it all.

▲ Designer:
Sarah Jo Warren,
aged 7
Judges' comment:
A brilliant design, which is not only about the Greenhouse Effect, but shows how the earth is like a fragile plant that needs protecting.

▶ Designer:
Lewis Fowler,
aged 6
Judges' comment:
Another stunningly good description of a global problem. The way the ozone layer is shown is especially good.

◀ Designer:
Alice Newton-Mold,
aged 12
Judges' comment:
A very graphic and effective way of getting the message across.

HANGING AROUND

Make yourself a piece of modern art! Mobiles are more than fun for babies: they are great ways of creating something out of the ordinary. We've got some ideas here, but ignore them if you like. Your mobile could be anything you want it to be. Once it's finished, watch it become alive as the air catches it.

The things we used:
washing-up bottle top
wire coathanger
thin string or thick cotton
paper plates
plastic bottle tops
egg carton
glue
scourer or vegetable netting
bendy drinking straws
paint (or colouring pencils)
sticky tape
card
plastic vegetable tray
paper clips
twine
garden sticks
shoe laces

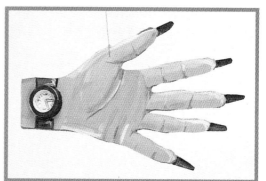

Start with the coathanger and tie three pieces of string to it. Paint two different faces, one on each plate. Use sections from the egg carton for noses, the pan scourer to make hair or moustaches. Bits of bendy straw make good eyebrows.

Dangling bow ties look great. Make them from cut-out triangles of paper plates, coloured in jazzy patterns.

Draw round your hands on card, cut out and paint. Again, do enough to have a back and a front view. Plastic from the vegetable tray painted red makes great fingernails. What about a paper-clip bracelet or a bottle-top watch? Stick each pair of hands together with twine in the middle.

Draw round your trainers to make shoes. Stick on some real shoe laces or paint one side as a bare, hairy foot. Godzilla!

Tie string from one hand and one foot to a garden stick, roughly three centimetres from each end. Sticky tape will stop the string sliding. Try to balance the stick so that it will hang straight when you tie it to the coathanger.

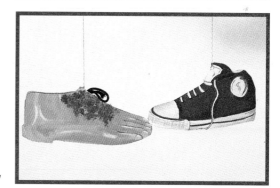

*Mobile designed by Paul Goddard from **Bitsa!***

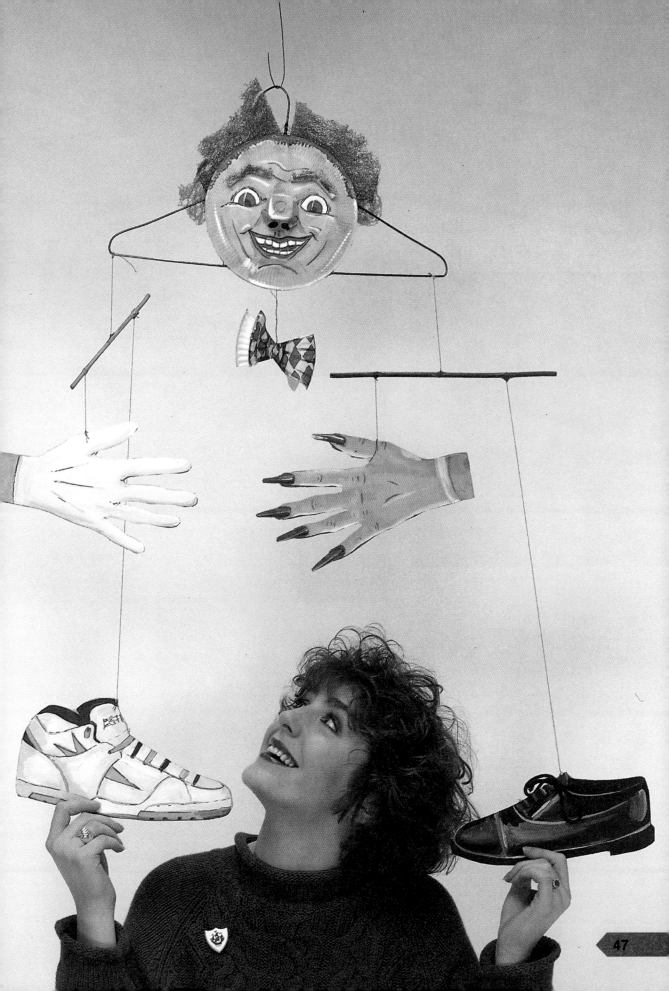

Clare Bradley
SUPERGARDENER!

Clare lives in Kew Palace, just right for a gardener.

Grow your own Sweet Peas

1. Soak the seeds overnight. Sow the fattest ones in pots made out of rolled-up newspaper!

2. Pinch out the top leaves before planting. Leave the newspaper. Place netting or twiggy branches for the plants to grow up.

3. Keep picking the flowers to make sure you have a display all summer. Once they form seeds, the plants will die – but you could save seeds for next year!

Sweet Pea
(Lathyrus odoratus)
Never-ending bunches of sweet-smelling flowers

Cornflower
(Centaurea cyanus)
Blue skies and a hot summer!

Field primrose
(Primula vulgaris)
A sure sign spring is coming!

Flame nettle
(Coleus blumei)
A technicolour dreamcoat, and easy to grow from cuttings

Sacred lotus
(Nelumbo nucifera)
The jewel in the crown!

Since Clare joined the Blue Peter team, the garden has never looked better!

She's absolutely full of bright ideas. One minute she's creating a compost zone, the next she's coming up with a scheme for the vegetable patch, and in between, she's pruned all the flowering shrubs! Clare's giant pumpkin competition brought about her only failure so far – our pumpkin seeds were planted too late, and the results were not very impressive!

Clare loves her new job. "I love being part of Blue Peter," says Clare, "because I can talk to the gardeners and conservationists of the future. It's also a lot of fun!"

Her biggest job to date has been trying to save the Tree for the Year 2000. Clare found the silver birch in very poor condition. She's put an emergency rescue plan into action, but there's only a slim chance she will be able to save the tree.

Plans for the future? "The garden has great potential! It had become rather overgrown and there's still more to do, but I'm enjoying the challenge! I want Blue Peter to be proud of its little green corner and to enjoy it!"

With Clare in charge, we'll all enjoy it.

CROSS-COUNTRY

Stylish cross-country skiing from the experts. Perhaps it's skiing uphill that makes it so muscle-sapping. The British junior team (right) are a force to be reckoned with. Ranging in age from 8 to 14, they certainly showed me a thing or two!

"I wasn't prepared for it ... I mean it didn't *look* that difficult..." blurted a breathless John at the end of the gruelling five-kilometre cross-country ski course.

High in the Bavarian Alps, John's first mistake was to watch the graceful, sliding motion of the cross-country skis on snow and think it was easy. On the contrary, it's often said that the cross-country skier is the fittest athlete of all, using ninety per cent of all energy resources. Add to that the thin air of the high alps and you have a recipe for exhaustion!

British team coach Ewan

SKIING

Struggling along the course. After a while, I was so tired that all co-ordination went. I knew I was doing it wrong, but I didn't have the strength to do it right!

Coach to the British juniors Ewan Mackenzie explained that it's a question of co-ordination and style. "Just glide," he said.

Mackenzie instructed John. "Imagine you're kicking a football," he advised, as John tried on the special cross-country skis – an easy instruction for *this* pupil to follow. Downhill was a cinch, uphill was less straight-forward. It took all John's strength just to stop sliding backwards!

On the flat, the long skating-like movements were gradually improving. Keen to put his new-found skills to the test, John signed up for the International Five Kilometre Classical Race that was taking place next day. In the under-12s class, he ought to stand a chance...

As John negotiated the course, he soon realised that he was no match for the 12-year-old whizz kids. Sheer grit took John across the finish line. "It's the only physical activity where I've felt that I had nothing left to give. Next time I'll be better prepared!"

I couldn't see the wood for the trees! And you can see my style looks pretty awful by this stage, which was about halfway along the course.

Thank heavens that's over! I'd rather face the Royal Marines Endurance Course any day! Next time I go skiing, it's going to be strictly downhill all the way!

In 1492, Columbus

S o goes the age old rhyme. There can't be many people who haven't heard of Christopher Columbus. His name conjures up romantic images of discovery, determination, bravery and glory. Countries, cities and even spacecraft have been named after this celebrated traveller. He sailed into the history books a hero, but is Columbus the character that history makes him out to be?

The real Christopher Columbus was convinced he could sail west to reach the Indies in the east. Diane played Chris in Blue Peter's reconstruction of the epic voyage on a park pond.

Columbus' flagship was the Santa Maria, a very small vessel by today's standards – about 24 metres long.

ailed the ocean blue...

It's five hundred years since Columbus "discovered" the "New World". His voyage was an act of enormous bravery. No one really knew what lay to the west but Columbus was convinced that it was possible to reach the riches of the Indies, China and Japan by sailing west instead of east. Unfortunately, he had calculated that the world was very much smaller than it actually was. When he finally set foot on land after his long and hard voyage, he wasn't in the Indies at all, he was in the Caribbean.

Columbus came from Genoa in Italy. He learned his trade in Portugal, where he became an accomplished voyager with a gift for chart or map making. It was a time of discovery, with adventurers pushing further and further into the unknown. In this atmosphere Columbus' ideas took shape.

His plan needed the support of a rich sponsor. Columbus began his search for backing by visiting King John of

TO PORTUGAL

> **This man is a sandwich short of a picnic!**

King John II

Portugal but the King turned him down.

Columbus was not put off. He went on to Spain, to the court of Queen Isabella. She was open to grand schemes that would add to the power and glory of Spain and spread the message of the Catholic Church, but Spain was at war and there was doubt that any ship could cope with such a long journey.

However, when the war was over, Columbus got the support he wanted. He went on to demand that he should be known as Admiral of the

TO SPAIN

Columbus struggled for years to convince people he wasn't mad and to raise the money for his voyage. King John of Portugal (top right) told him to get lost, but eventually Queen Isabella of Spain (right) backed him.

> **And if there's any gold going, I'll be getting it!**

Columbus had to cope not only with not knowing where he was going...

Columbus was pleased with the results of his voyage but the Carib peoples would live to regret the arrival of Europeans.

Ocean Sea and Viceroy of the new lands claimed for Spain, as well as getting a cut of any riches he discovered. Reluctantly, Queen Isabella agreed.

Columbus gathered his resources and hired three ships and a crew. Enough provisions and bulky fresh water for a year were loaded, along with beads and trinkets as gifts for the natives they might come across. The fleet was ready to set sail.

Columbus, on board the *Santa Maria*, kept a record of his travels. Life was tough on the Ocean Sea. The seamen had no sleeping quarters –

...but also with his crew. Most of them thought he was leading them the wrong way.

The longer the voyage became, the less they trusted him.

N

E

S

they would just grab forty winks somewhere on deck. Food was little better: a miserable diet of dry biscuits and occasional rotten stews.

The voyage began on August 3rd. By October 10th, with no land in sight, the crew had lost all their trust in Columbus and were ready to mutiny. He persuaded them to carry on for another three days. The following day the sight that everyone had been waiting for appeared in the mist – land! The relief was indescribable but neither Columbus nor his crew could begin to understand what they had achieved.

That landing opened not only a new avenue of trade but a new era in human history, and it was to mean as much loss as discovery. As Europeans explored more and more of the islands of the "New World" in the wake of Columbus, they brought with them diseases and armies that wiped out whole populations. It led to peoples being crushed and the development of slavery. For the population of the Caribbean, Columbus' arrival meant anything but discovery; it meant invasion. Furthermore, his expedition may not have been the first European landing on the

Caribbean shores in any case. Irish monks, among others, were said to have landed several centuries earlier.

The 1992 view of Columbus is rather different from the traditional descriptions of a glorious discoverer. But he did change the world. He took *his* world and set it on its path to becoming the place we know today. Strangely, he went to his grave without knowing that he had found two vast new continents. His life was a dramatic tale but perhaps not a heroic one. It was not a story of one person but of many people.

Mrs Edwards still has plenty of animals down on her farm – even if her main crop is electricity!

CATCH THE WIND!

What's growing down on the farm? Potatoes? Radishes? Not any more! The crop on the Edwards' family farm in North Cornwall is electricity!

The Edwards live in one of the windiest parts of Britain. Instead of letting all those gale force 8s go to waste, they've copied the Dutch and the Scandinavians and worked out a way to harvest the wind. Their ten giant new windmills use the power of the wind to run a turbine and generate electricity.

John went to explore these modern windmills. As you can see from the pictures, they don't look a bit like the traditional ones. These look more like giant aircraft propellors mounted on enormous flagpoles. The masts are hollow. John climbed up inside to see the complicated cogs and gears that link the blades to the turbine.

The ten windmills between them make enough power to serve 3,000 homes. It must be nice to turn on the light and know you're helping the environment. And it's even nicer to know that landlubbers have finally found something to do with the wind besides drying the washing!

Each wind turbine's supporting tower was erected in two giant pieces and the turbine house fits on top. The wind blades are bolted to

the driveshaft, which connects through a gearbox to the generator, which makes electricity when the wind blows. Easy!

John had to climb the long ladder to reach the turbine house – it was pretty windy up there! The blades can take more than a gale force wind though. In fact they can withstand winds of 140mph.

John Leslie is 6' 5" but it would need seventeen of him to reach the top of one windmill!

To anyone interested in a greener future (and who isn't?) this is a very bright idea. Wind-generated power is clean electricity. No clouds of nasty gases are produced; no acid rain is created. What's more, wind-power will not run out – especially in North Cornwall! That's more than can be said for oil, gas or coal. You need a lot of windmills to make enough electricity to replace even one coal-fired power station. Even so, in ten years' time, about ten per cent of Britain's electricity could come from the wind.

Information from Friends of the Earth.

Welcome back 532 Blue Peter

The 60532 in full steam in December 1991 on the North Yorkshire Moors Railway (above), just days after the renaming ceremony performed by Diane. If you look carefully (right), you can see the name of the 60532's original owners on the brass cabside works plate – the London North Eastern Railway. Just one week after the loco entered service in 1948, the railways were nationalised and the LNER disappeared for ever!

60532

December 11th 1991 was a big day for all steam locomotive enthusiasts. That was when one of the last giants of the days of steam made a welcome comeback, fully restored and ready to haul trains again.

The 60532 Blue Peter is a Class A-2 Pacific locomotive. Named after the racehorse that won the 1939 Derby, she spent the years from 1948 to 1966 carrying passengers, but once steam locomotives were replaced by diesels, she was left to rot.

She was rescued by Geoff Drury in 1968 and lovingly

restored, a process followed on Blue Peter. If your parents are fans of the programme, perhaps they remember the amazing scenes at Doncaster in 1970 when sixty thousand people watched the presenters at the renaming ceremony.

The 1991 ceremony was a quieter affair! Diane went to Wilton, where the Blue Peter has once more been fully restored. The work has been done by the North Eastern Locomotive Preservation Group with help from ICI. Five years of hard labour, including complete refurbishment of the boilers, has paid off – the loco has probably never looked better since the day she left the Doncaster works in 1948. As a tribute to the fine work of the restorers, the NELPG won the Premier Award in the 1992 Steam Heritage Awards.

No. 60532 Blue Peter was straight off to work. For the

Diane enjoyed her stint as fireman, shovelling coal into the furnace to feed the fire and keep the steam up. The newly restored footplate (right) is a steam engineer's dream.

first time since 1966, she's able to haul a full train of passengers. She's now the most powerful working steam loco in Britain, capable of pulling twelve or thirteen carriages and has reached speeds of 83mph during tests on British Rail track. She's one of a pool of steam locos that run special trains along famous scenic lines such as the Settle to Carlisle route that runs through the Pennines.

If you are one of Britain's thousands of steam lovers, perhaps you will one day have the chance to ride in a carriage being pulled by one of the most powerful locos ever to run the tracks. And thanks to the loving work put in by restorers like Geoff Drury, Maurice Burns and his colleagues in the NELPG, the magnificent sight of a loco in full steam will never be shut away in the history books, but will live on in years to come.

The return of 60532 Blue Peter was featured on the front cover of Railway Magazine.

FEBRUARY 1992 £1.85

Railway
MAGAZINE

ed since 1897

REE TWO CLASSIC PRINTS

rking with the 50s

ETURN OF 'BLUE PETER'

Class 465 launched

Steam on the Manx Electric

Alfred County Railway

CrossRail latest

ABC of RfD

Fact Box

- 60532 Blue Peter carries 5,000 gallons of water and 9 tonnes of coal. She uses about 6 tonnes during a full 150-mile run.
- There were 14 Class A-2 Pacific locomotives.
- They were all named after racehorses.
- Her colour is known as "British Rail dark green express passenger livery".
- In BR service, the Blue Peter worked the Waterloo – Exeter line, and spent her final years in Scotland.

HOW TO WIN A Blue Peter

Badge

SILVERbadges are awarded to people who have already won a Blue badge. You have to do something different to win your Silver, so if you've already sent us a poem, you will have to think of something else to win a Silver. Remember our address for letters is: Blue Peter, BBC TV, London W12 7RJ.

GREENbadges were first awarded a few years ago to show how interested many children are in the environment. If you send us a story, poem, song or your view about any "green" subject, you could win a Green badge. Let us know what you have been doing to help the world around you.

BLUEbadges are the ones the presenters normally wear. You could win one for sending us an idea for the programme, an interesting letter, a recipe, a poem or a story. If you ever *appear* on the programme, you will automatically win a Blue badge. Like all our badges, it gives you free entry to about a hundred attractions all over Britain (and even one in Holland!).

COMPETITIONbadges are awarded to winners and runners-up. You have more chance than you might think of winning one of these. When we run a really big competition, like the Expo '92 or Royal Mail Green Stamps ones, we have a thousand (sometimes *two* thousand) runners-up. So keep entering! Our competition address is: Blue Peter, PO Box 20, BBC TV, London W12 6BP.

GOLDbadges are rarely awarded. They are only given to people for outstanding feats of bravery – like saving someone's life. (We need proof!) We decide who will receive a Gold badge – you cannot "earn" one by winning our other badges.

ANSWERS

Plunderful pirates! (pages 8–9)

Fact and Fiction
Fact: Statement 5 is fiction. The *Hispaniola* is the name of the ship in *Treasure Island*.
Fiction: Statement 2 is true!

The Great Blue Peter Trivia Challenge (pages 40–41)

1 Edinburgh **2** Yvette **3** Yvette and John **4** Caron and Yvette
5 19,000,000 **6** Honey, Biddy, Major, Lily, Teddy and Margot **7** £6,500,000
8 Biddy Baxter **9** Mark Curry or Caron Keating **10** Valerie Singleton
11 Simon Groom **12** Rose Bruford
13 A-2 Pacific (no marks for "steam")
14 Her ancient Morris Minor (deceased) **15** Chalk Farm Band of the Salvation Army (½ mark for Salvation Army) **16** The Magnolias
17 Flag raised by a ship twenty-four hours before leaving port **18** Peter Duncan **19** Janet Ellis **20** Yvette
21 Five extra marks if you got this one. The 1939 Derby was won by a horse called Blue Peter. Fairway and Fancy Free were its parents!

Some useful information

Blue Peter
BBC TV
London
W12 7RJ

Aluminium Can Recycling Association
I-MEX House
52 Blucher Street
Birmingham
B1 1QU

British Amateur Gymnastics Association
Suites 035–037
Holiday Inn London-Heathrow
Stockley Road
West Drayton
Middlesex
UB7 9NA

British Ski Federation
258 Main Street
East Calder
West Lothian
EH53 0EE

Friends of the Earth
Energy Campaign
26–28 Underwood Street
London
N1 7JQ

Help the Aged
St James's Walk
London
EC1R 0BE

National Star Fleet Alliance
Star Trek Fan Clubs
7 Edgewell Close
Foxhill
Sheffield
S6 1FF
(send s.a.e.)

532 Blue Peter
North Eastern
Locomotive Preservation
Group
c/o 5 Blackfriars
Yarm
Cleveland
TS15 9HQ

John Nike Leisure Sports Complex
John Nike Way
Amen Corner
Binfield
Near Bracknell
Berkshire
RG12 4TN

Thunderbirds
The Fanderson Junior
Fan Club
PO Box 93
Wakefield
West Yorkshire
WF1 1XJ
(send s.a.e.)

Wood Green Animal Shelters
Chishall Road
Heydon
Near Royston
Hertfordshire
SG8 8PN